SPRING VALLEY

DOGS SET VII

GOLDENDOODLES

Jill C. Wheeler
ABDO Publishing Company

visit us at
www.abdopublishing.com

Published by ABDO Publishing Company, 8000 West 78th Street, Edina, Minnesota 55439. Copyright © 2008 by Abdo Consulting Group, Inc. International copyrights reserved in all countries. No part of this book may be reproduced in any form without written permission from the publisher. The Checkerboard Library™ is a trademark and logo of ABDO Publishing Company.

Printed in the United States.

Cover Photo: Chelle Rohde Calbert/www.designerdoggies.com
Interior Photos: Chelle Rohde Calbert/www.designerdoggies.com pp. 5, 13, 15, 19, 21;
    Moss Creek Goldendoodles of Florida pp. 10, 11, 14, 16, 17; Peter Arnold pp. 7, 9

Editors: Heidi M.D. Elston, Megan M. Gunderson
Art Direction: Neil Klinepier

Library of Congress Cataloging-in-Publication Data

Wheeler, Jill C., 1964-
  Goldendoodles / Jill C. Wheeler.
     p. cm. -- (Dogs. Set VII)
  Includes index.
  ISBN 978-1-59928-963-2
  1. Goldendoodle--Juvenile literature. I. Title.

  SF429.G64W44 2008
  636.72--dc22
                                    2007031518

CONTENTS

What Kind of Dog Is That?

Adopting a dog is a big decision. There are hundreds of dog **breeds** to choose from. So for many people, it is also a hard decision.

Dogs and humans have worked together for about 12,000 years. The first dogs were wolf pups tamed to help ancient peoples hunt. Wolves and modern dogs are part of the Canidae **family**.

Today, designer dogs have many people talking. Breeding two different **purebred** dogs together creates designer dogs.

Purebred dog lovers often disapprove of these crossbred dogs. They claim people are being charged too much money for a mutt. But, mixed-breed dog

Many goldendoodle owners happily call their dogs "doodles."

lovers disagree. They say mixing **breeds** leads to healthier dogs. And, they believe the dogs better suit the needs and wants of their owners.

For many owners, that is true of goldendoodles. Goldendoodles are a mix of golden retrievers and poodles.

GOLDEN RETRIEVERS

The golden retriever is the fourth most popular dog **breed** in the United States. The breed began in Scotland in the late 1800s. Hunters wanted a medium-sized dog that could retrieve birds from land and water.

In 1868, Lord Tweedmouth bred a yellow wavy-coated retriever with a tweed water spaniel. Tweedmouth later added the Irish setter and bloodhound breeds into his mix.

The golden retriever breed made its way to North America in the 1920s. It was first registered by the **American Kennel Club (AKC)** in 1925.

Golden retrievers are intelligent, friendly dogs. They make excellent family pets. As adults, they are patient and devoted to their owners. And, they are popular as guide dogs for the blind.

In addition, today's golden retrievers are skilled hunting dogs. They also do well in obedience training and **agility** tests.

These high-energy dogs love nothing more than to spend the day playing with their owners.

POODLES

Like golden retrievers, poodles are highly popular dogs. Many people think of poodles as pampered pets with fancy haircuts. In reality, poodles began as hunting and working dogs. They arrived in the United States in the late 1800s. The **AKC** first recognized the **breed** in 1887.

Poodles come in three sizes. Standard poodles are the largest and the calmest. Miniature poodles are the next smallest size. Toy poodles are the smallest of the three.

Poodles are smart and easy to train. So, they have been favorites of circuses and traveling performers. Their ability to learn tricks made them popular among European royalty, too. Poodles are also good for families with children and other pets.

The poodle's coat has added to its popularity, especially when **breeding** designer dogs. Most dogs have hair that grows a bit then falls out, or sheds. But poodle coats grow long unless trimmed, much like human hair. This means poodles shed less. That is good news for people who are allergic to fur but want a dog.

Poodles are among the AKC's top ten most popular dog breeds.

GOLDENDOODLE STORY

People began **breeding** goldendoodles in the 1990s. Usually, the name is credited to golden retriever breeder Amy Lane of West Virginia. When one of her male golden retrievers died, Lane replaced him with a male poodle. She bred the new poodle to one of her prize golden retrievers.

Goldendoodle mothers usually have their babies about 57 days after mating. The puppies are born blind and deaf.

A high-quality diet is an important step to giving puppies a good start in life.

Lane named the resulting puppies goldendoodles for their light, fluffy coats. What excited Lane most was the reaction she got from families adopting goldendoodles. People loved that these gentle, smart pets either did not shed or shed very little.

GOLDENDOODLES

Purebred puppies come from multiple generations. That makes all puppies of a particular **breed** similar in looks and in health. Each parent passes on the same genes to their puppies. So if the parents have health problems, the puppies will likely inherit those same problems.

Many people believe that designer dogs are healthier than purebred dogs. Each parent introduces different genes to their puppies. So, the puppies are less likely to inherit undesirable **traits**. Still, it is impossible to control which genes are passed on and which are not.

Goldendoodles are not a breed, so their appearances can vary. Most goldendoodles have the strong legs and the high-set ears of the golden

retriever. Usually, a goldendoodle's nose is more like a poodle nose. It is longer and narrower than the nose of a golden retriever.

The goldendoodle exhibits the friendly nature of the golden retriever and the low-shedding coat of the poodle. What a perfect combination!

BEHAVIOR

Many people love goldendoodles because goldendoodles love people. Goldendoodle owners must provide their dogs with plenty of attention. They need a lot of time with people.

Goldendoodles do not like to be left alone for long. They are smart dogs and can become bored. That boredom

Puppies like to chew! So, owners need to provide their goldendoodles with dog toys.

Doodles are calm and friendly. So generally, they are good around children.

may lead to unwanted behaviors, such as chewing on things they shouldn't.

Goldendoodles are not territorial. This means they tend not to be upset by strangers or other pets. And usually, they are quiet dogs.

Like their parent **breeds**, goldendoodles enjoy retrieving games. They also love water. Goldendoodles are easy to train. This quality and their love of people make them perfect guide dogs. Some goldendoodles have also been trained as sniffer dogs.

COATS & COLORS

Goldendoodles may shed a little or not at all. Some **breeders** cross a goldendoodle that sheds with a poodle. This is called a backcross. Puppies from these **litters** will likely

Owners should bathe their doodles only when necessary. Overbathing can dry out the skin and the coat.

shed less than their goldendoodle parent.

Goldendoodle coats can range from the soft, wavy fluff of a golden retriever coat to the tight curls of a poodle coat. The hair can be four to eight inches (10 to 20 cm) long.

A goldendoodle needs daily brushing and combing. That way, the coat does not mat or tangle. Also, a goldendoodle with a poodlelike coat needs regular clipping.

Most goldendoodles come in gold colors. Yet that can vary depending on the color of the poodle parent. Goldendoodles have been **bred** in cream, apricot, red, black, blue, and even chocolate. Some goldendoodle coats lighten with age.

A goldendoodle's regular grooming should include trimming the nails and cleaning the ears.

SIZES

The first goldendoodles had golden retriever and standard poodle parents. Later, **breeders** began using miniature and toy poodles as well. Most golden retrievers are about the same size. So, a goldendoodle's size depends on the size of its poodle parent.

Goldendoodles with a standard poodle parent stand 20 to 24 inches (51 to 61 cm) tall. They weigh 50 to 80 pounds (23 to 36 kg), depending on if they are male or female. Males are larger.

Goldendoodles with a miniature poodle parent stand 17 to 20 inches (43 to 51 cm) tall. They weigh between 40 and 50 pounds (18 and 23 kg).

Toy poodle parents produce the smallest goldendoodles. These dogs stand up to 20 inches (51 cm) tall. They weigh 15 to 35 pounds (7 to 16 kg).

Larger goldendoodles can have either **breed** as the mother. But for miniature and toy goldendoodles, the golden retriever should always be the mother.

Goldendoodle puppies can double in size between 8 and 16 weeks of age!

CARE

Like all dogs, goldendoodles need regular visits to a veterinarian. Goldendoodle puppies need vaccinations to prevent common canine diseases. They should also be **spayed** or **neutered** at the proper age. Usually, this is before they reach six months old.

Goldendoodle owners need to be on the lookout for health issues. Both poodles and golden retrievers frequently have eye and hip problems. Goldendoodle **breeders** try to use dogs that do not have these problems. However, not all problems can be spotted in advance.

Finally, goldendoodles need a healthy diet, fresh water, and moderate amounts of daily exercise. Owners who take good care of their goldendoodles can expect them to live for 10 to 15 years.

Goldendoodles need a leash, a collar, identification tags, toys, bedding, and lots of love.

GLOSSARY

agility - the ability to move quickly and easily.

American Kennel Club (AKC) - an organization that studies and promotes interest in purebred dogs.

breed - a group of animals sharing the same appearance and characteristics. A breeder is a person who raises animals. Raising animals is often called breeding them.

family - a group that scientists use to classify similar plants or animals. It ranks above a genus and below an order.

litter - all of the puppies born at one time to a mother dog.

neuter - to remove a male animal's reproductive organs.

purebred - an animal whose parents are both from the same breed.

spay - to remove a female animal's reproductive organs.

trait - a quality that distinguishes one group from another.

WEB SITES

To learn more about designer dogs, visit ABDO
Publishing Company on the World Wide Web at
www.abdopublishing.com. Web sites about designer
dogs are featured on our Book Links page. These links
are routinely monitored and updated to provide the
most current information available.

INDEX